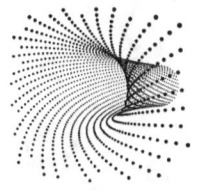

FIRSTMATTERPRESS

Portland, Ore.

STORIES
FOR
WHEN
THE
WOLVES
ARRIVE

STORIES FOR WHEN THE WOLVES ARRIVE

hailey spencer

FIRSTMATTERPRESS

Portland, Ore.

Copyright © 2022 by Hailey Spencer
All rights reserved

First Edition

Published in the United States
by First Matter Press
Portland, Oregon

Paperback ISBN 978-1-958600-00-9

Lead Editor: Lauren Paredes
Contributing Editors: Natalie Garyet, Ben Read,
Caroline Wilcox Reul, Ash Good & Emily Moon

First Matter Press Cohort Collaborators:
Riley Danvers, Xylophone Mykland,
Sonya Wohletz & ahuva s. zaslavsky

Cover Illustration: *A Dead Mother's Hands*
Copyright © 2022 by Rachel Mulder
rchlmldr.com

Book Design: Ash Good
ashgood.com

For Elizabeth,
and everything she said to me about Cinderella
before we fell in love.

CONTENTS

Interlude One

The Heart's Trap

Interlude Two

The Journey Home

INTRODUCTION

I can still remember the heft of my childhood copy of *The Classic Fairy Tale Treasury*. I had two similar books that accompanied it: a children's collection of Hans Christian Andersen stories and a world folklore collection that I've tried and failed to track down. I read these books for hours, laid out on my bedroom floor immersed in the words and pictures. *The Classic Fairy Tale Treasury* has a brownish cover depicting a forest in autumn, a smiling blonde fairy, a skipping dwarf (who I can only assume is Rumpelstiltskin), and a dozen other folklore characters who smile as they walk through the woods. I don't know if the pages were actually gilded, but that's how I remember them.

It wasn't until I started writing this collection that I began to look beyond the stories themselves and into the rich body of research that accompanies them. There are many approaches to folklore scholarship, but of everything I read, the most influential to this collection was the role of trauma in fairy tales. Scholars have noted the repetitive nature of fairy tales, and connected this attribute to the process of trauma and recovery. In narrative therapy, the retelling of the traumatic event as a story can be one tool to regain control. In the arrangement of these poems, I focused on the narrative of trauma and recovery, and the way that fairy tales speak heavily on both.

In addition to the more psychological approach, this collection of poems relies heavily on the Aarne-Thompson-Uther (ATU) Index. Originally designed in 1910 by Finnish folklorist Antti Aarne, the system has since been updated; first in 1928 by American folklorist Stith Thompson, and later in 2004 by German folklorist Hans-Jörg Uther. The ATU Index is used to classify folktales cross-culturally, finding connections between similar stories from different parts of the world as well as organizing folktales by content. With specific criteria for which motifs must be included, it becomes possible to categorize stories, and therefore examine their connections. The ATU system is helpful for anyone looking to deepen their understanding of folk and fairy tales.

While the ATU system may seem diametrically opposed to the more psychological approach, I believe they are two sides of the same coin. For whatever reason, fairy tales matter to us collectively. Many of these stories have existed for hundreds or even thousands of years, across many iterations. Some people choose to ask what effect they have on our psyche. Others try to trace history, lineage, motifs. To me, both are attempts to understand why these stories have such a hold on us. Delightfully, there is no clear answer. We do not know why fairy tales matter, only that they do. The ATU index condenses stories to pure structure and motif. Even in these strange, truncated forms, the stories spoke to me. As a poet, I found this fascinating.

In this collection, I work with 19 different fairy tales over the course of 57 poems. 15 of these stories represent different tale types. The remaining four are ATU 510A stories, best known by American audiences as Cinderella stories. This tale type, often referred to as

"The Persecuted Heroine," is one of the oldest and most prevalent in the world. The selection of 510A stories here is in no way definitive, as scholars estimate that over 2,000 versions of this story exist worldwide. I chose the tales that spoke most to the overarching narrative of this collection. The country of origin for these stories is listed next to the title of the first poem in the set. For every folktale in this book, the corresponding ATU number can be found at the bottom of the page. For those interested in searching by ATU number, an appendix on page 117 lists the tale-type numbers in order, as well as the exact story and translation that I used as my primary source for each poem. Additional research and personal notes can be found on page 120.

While I have frontloaded some scholarly information here, this book is not a poetic analysis of the fairy tale. I wrote it because the magic of fairy tales has trailed me throughout my life in ways I am still unearthing. Children's shows of Baba Yaga stories at the puppet theater near my elementary school. The edgy middle school phase of telling everyone the "true" stories of these fairy tales—chopped off toes, cannibalism of the grandmother's remains, whatever morbid versions I could find. I read twisted, fractured fairy tales and tried to write my own. It wasn't that I wanted to be a princess. If anything, I may have wanted to be the witch.

It is easy to explain this childhood love and harder to explain why these stories have such a strong grip on me into adulthood. The Baba Yaga of Slavic folklore gives children impossible tasks, and their completion determines if the child will be cannibalized or blessed. Revealing my heart on this matter means following the footprints to her house and awaiting this same judgment. The best I can say is this: there is humanity in these stories that transcends time and culture, if you're willing to follow the breadcrumb path and shoo away the birds. I hope that within these pages you will find the same magic I found as a young girl balancing a giant book on my knees. I hope that you will find the light-filled autumn forest, and its moonlit mirror filled with wolves and oni. I hope you will go through the woods and come out different on the other side.

—Hailey Spencer, April 2022

A PATH
THROUGH
THE
WOODS

The Children With the Witch

1. A mother and father abandon their children in the woods.

The pebbled pathway leads to a simple cottage. The glass is spun sugar and the mortar made from icing. It is the only food they've seen in weeks, aside from stale crumbs of bread finished hours ago and mostly left to the sparrows.

The boy licks the glass while the girl bites down on the walls.

2. They are kidnapped by a witch.

Nobody safe lives in the woods. Nobody safe lives in a house in the woods. Nobody safe lives in a house made of sweets in the woods.

There is no such thing as safe.

3. The witch prepares to eat them.

The boy tries to stay small, bony and unpleasant on the tongue. With every bite he swears that it's his last. But there is only so much you can teach an empty body about starvation. His fingers are pink with peppermint.

4. The children escape.

After shoving the witch into the oven, the children devour the remains of the house, filling themselves until they have entirely forgotten the crumbs that came before.

ATU 327A

Sugarcoated

Two children sprinkle breadcrumbs down a path.
Fear chokes them, but they force themselves to laugh.

They find a house with gumdrop windowpanes.
They fill their stomachs and their terror wanes.

And then: a witch, protruding bones and greed.
Her house, mere bait for those on whom she'll feed.

But one child tricks the witch, cooks her instead.
They sneak home through the window into bed.

(And what will happen when their parents wake?
Back to the woods, their ginger hearts to break?)

Breadcrumbs

Crows pick at amethyst berries
as her own ravenous stomach betrays itself with sound.
Her pockets full of stones she never bothered to sow

there are some things her brother does not know.

Such as: the moth, which even now
alights on the oak to lay its eggs
but has no mouth of its own.

Or two children, headed home to this:

a broken father, their mother's shuttered arms.
Love, perhaps, hidden in the cellar
or the attic cracks, but more importantly

barren cupboards

a breadbox full of pebbles.

The Sleeping Princess

1. A fairy casts a curse on a young princess.

With no spindles in the kingdom, production comes to a halt. The king's velvet cloak grows stiff and unsmooth. The queen's veil is covered with pockmarks. The tailors tear the curtains from the princess's canopy to sew her ballroom gown.

2. The princess falls into a hundred-year sleep.

In her dream, she carries a spindle between her hands. She wanders through the woods as she works, spinning a long golden chain. For fear of losing it, she uses a sailor's knot to anchor one end to her ankle.

3. A prince awakens her with a kiss.

She screams, but the rest of the kingdom is still waking.

She can no longer remember the dream, only fragments that occasionally light up in her mind like pebbles under moonlight.

4. They are married that same day.

Afterwards, when the prince is asleep in their bed, the princess wanders the castle. Those who come across her in her nightgown, with gray and brittle hair, believe they have seen a ghost.

In the mornings, these encounters go unmentioned.

ATU 410

The Spindle and the Sleep

This story of a princess who, in sleep,
fell into dreams carnivorous and deep.
Those grey-soaked days, when all she did was weep.

A dozen fairies saw her birthing cry
but one in anger raised her wand up high.
Her curse: at age sixteen the girl would die.

Another of the guests cast through her tears
a spell that fell on many grateful ears:
she would not die, but sleep one hundred years.

So when the princess reached that dreaded age
she wandered through the halls and met a sage.
This crone was spinning threads of finest gauge.

The princess pricked her finger, took a fall
and landed on a bed. Around its walls
the castle grew a thicket, firm and tall.

For years, proud princes worked hard to break in.
Swords pierced the brambles, almost there, but then
the thicket thickened and they could not win.

The time arrives: a new prince and a kiss.
The princess wakes into a certain bliss:
back to a life she hadn't known to miss.

That evening they are married in the hall:
a feast, a frock, a dance, a royal ball.
The princess says she doesn't mind at all.

Doesn't Mind at All

A chrysalis wrapped up in silken dreams
longs to dissolve inside herself——

blue twilight through the woods,
a body that is not
her body.

Even the careful steps of spiders
against the skin of her wrist
cannot make her emerge.

It is only the rustle of brambles
against glass that wakes her,
soft vibrations through her chest.

She does not know when in this story she is.

A spindle sharp against her finger.
Silk spun tight around her throat.

The Name

1. A king demands a girl turn straw to gold.

The straw has been left to rot in the rain. She tears into it, but it offers no clues, only larvae and six dozen spider legs. The chapel door is locked from the outside.

2. A dwarf offers to do the work in exchange for the girl's firstborn child.

While he spins, she lies down in the hay and tries to sleep. She had a dream once about a spinning wheel, but she can't remember how it ended.

She awakens on a pile of gold. Her body has left its imprint in the soft strands. When the king unlocks the door, a smile crawls across his face.

3. The dwarf offers a new deal: learn his name, and keep her child.

Unable to marry the gold itself, the king settles for the woman who has spun it. But gold does not make a good bed. Gold does not make a safe home or a kind husband or an unlocked door.

Their baby lies under metal blankets and screams himself to sleep.

4. The girl tells the dwarf his name is Rumpelstiltskin.

The gold ring on her finger dissolves, leaving nothing but the smell of decay. The baby is safe in her arms. The dwarf is gone.

ATU 500

Straw for Gold

There once was a girl with a father
whose lies left her trapped in a room
to spin straw into gold—what a bother!—
her fingers scratched dry by the loom.

At midnight the girl lies there sleeping,
when out of thin air he arrives:
a dwarf with a beard long and creeping
and laughter right up to his eyes.

He asks her what she has to offer.
Her eyes roll at the creature's cliché.
There isn't a coin in her coffer,
no trinket to trade to this fay.

He grins and his teeth shimmer crudely—
a diamond atop of a ring.
There's an answer here if she thinks shrewdly.
The girl stops and considers the king,

whose knife lies in wait, sharp and wavy
with hopes that she'll fail at his task.
The dwarf names his price: her first baby.
It's not an impossible ask.

She awakes to a room filled with treasure
and in burst the king and his men.
He fingers the gold with sharp pleasure.
She takes a deep breath, counts to ten.

She marries the king. Some months later,
a son is wrapped up in her arms.
She rocks him and tries not to wait for—
just then the guards sound the alarm.

In lieu of their previous contract,
the dwarf offers her a new game.
He'll leave and have no further contact
in three days, if she guesses his name.

The morning the girl solves this riddle,
she clutches her child to her chest.
At her husband's shrewd gaze her heart whittles—
and surely you know all the rest.

Loom

1. Beds of straw and beds of gold. Women who spin and cannot be still. The name of the helper. The name of the blackmailer. Coffins of straw and coffins of gold. The spinning wheel's invention in the fourteenth century. The drop spindle, documented as existing as far back as the first century.

2. The gold chain around her neck and the invisible ones on her wrists. The nauseous smell of metal on her finger. Spinning as a social activity, performed alongside stories in the evening. The industrial revolution and the transubstantiation of the fabric industry into the hands of men. The origin of the word "spinster."

3. Cutting the thread of life in one tight snip. Blades that dull from overuse on metal. The moment of death, as determined by the work of women

    or in this case, a dwarf.

The Maiden in the Tower

1. A man promises his unborn daughter to a witch.

He watches as the tower is erected. It ought to take a hundred men a year, but when the witch touches the stones they rise up to the heavens.

2. In her prison, she lets down her hair for the witch and a prince to climb.

Sometimes when the witch arrives, the girl tries to say no. Later, when another begins his ascent, she finally half-desires the tug against her scalp. As he grows higher, strands of hair begin to pull painfully apart at the follicle.

She saves them in a box beneath her pillow.

3. The witch, learning the truth, blinds the prince and exiles the girl.

A desert in the midst of the woods, empty of anything to pray to except for the sky. The trees close in on all four sides. They look like home and feel like a pair of arms holding her tightly. It's hard to say whether this is an embrace or a restraint.

Her hair has been chopped unevenly, so she finishes the work, removing each strand from the root until her scalp is bare.

ATU 310

4. *The couple is reunited. The maiden's tears restore*
    the prince's sight.

In the mornings, she wakes up with a head that is far too easy to lift.
It would be wrong to say she misses the weight, so she doesn't.

A Flower Enshrined

It starts inside the garden wall:
a girl named for a flower
is traded for her father's life
and locked inside a tower.

Outside the tower lie the woods
that wander through her dreams.
She dreams of going deep inside
beneath the moonlit gleam.

But every day at half-past noon
the witch comes riding by,
demands the girl let down her hair
and climbs her way inside.

For years it's this, without a change,
until at one day's break
a new voice calls "Let down your hair!"
and startles her awake.

She lets it down. She lets him in,
this man, the first she's seen.
And when he leaves, she sees him go—
out past the forest green.

And every day, when he rides by
she watches from above.
He keeps her distant company.
They slowly fall in love.

The witch learns what the girl has done
(as witches always do)
and sends her to to the desert, dry,
its sky a poison blue.

This place is not a tower, and
this place is not the woods.
It's lonely, but without the witch
she thinks it might be good.

So in this place she waits and walks
and in this place she learns.
She lies awake, delighted dread
awaiting love's return.

Beneath the Moonlit Gleam

She sings sometimes,
awake in a round room, enveloped in
twin fists of clay and stone

No way out, no way in unless she
chooses to let down her matted hair.

(She's tried so hard to keep it clean and brushed.)

Princes and witches are her only visitors;
this is her castle, no doors and stairs
no bedrooms on the floors below, just space——

but in dreams she wanders winding paths
through wolves and trees, towards
cotton-candy cottages with doors too flimsy

for her grasping hands.

The Glutton

1. A girl sets off through the woods toward her grandmother's house.

The story: a young girl brings sweets to an ailing relative. We can see a sketch of the house emerge in the background, its colors not yet filled in. We wonder if she will make it by nightfall.

2. A wolf asks where she is going. She tells him where her grandmother lives.

The moral: never talk to strangers in the woods.

Her bouquet brims in her arms, leaving a trail of petals behind her on the path.

3. The girl reaches the house and finds the wolf in her grandmother's clothes.

What big eyes she had, what big ears she had, what big teeth she had. Nobody could ever be fooled by such a disguise. You are and will always be safe, as long as you can see the teeth.

4. The wolf eats the girl.

Stomach acid is a poor substitute for air. The blood on the cloak is damp but leaves no stain.

5. (Optional) A hunter comes by and rescues the girl.

After all, nobody really dies in the woods.

The Wolf

Walking the woods with a red hooded cape,
comes a girl with a basket of sweets.
The girl, she is kind, and the girl, she is good
and she's coated in sweat from the heat.

She's stopped by a wolf who comes sniffing about
and asks where she's going today.
She gives him directions, leaves nothing to doubt
and he goes there his own secret way.

The wolf soon finds Granny asleep in her bed
and he asks in his most childish voice,
"Oh Granny, you there, are you sick, are you dead?"
And she lets him in by her own choice.

He swallows her whole, tucks himself in to wait
as the girl comes along down the trail.
She enters the door, firmly sealing her fate.
When she sees him she feels herself pale.

"What big arms—what big eyes—what big teeth—"
the girl gasps, understanding a moment too late.
Now he's eaten her too, a devouring too brief
for his hunger to truly abate.

The wolf's now asleep in this house in the woods.
Soon a hunter comes ambling along,
slits the throat of the wolf, saves the girl with the hood,
and then strolls away humming a song.

The girl and her granny, now partially dissolved,
have been freed from the dangerous beast.
The girl skips back home, their adventure resolved,
and she grins with her now fang-like teeth.

A Devouring Too Brief

The only freedom from summer's obscene heat
lies down the garden path towards the woods.
Her mother shutters the windows to block out the view.

The girl reminds her that the wolf is dead.
The cloying wildflowers drift inside the door.
It takes all her might to resist.

At night, she dreams of running through the woods.
In the dark, the claw prints on her thighs
resemble the spindly fingers of the evergreens.

Light bleeds in through the branches
and each day the girl gives herself
another centimeter to explore.

INTERLUDE
ONE

The Persecuted Heroine (Japanese)

1. A girl is abused by her family.

The demands never cease: a bag full of chestnuts, crimson dishes, a house without a single speck of dust. They hope she will die in the woods, worms crawling their way out of her mouth.

2. The girl seeks magical assistance.

Go to the woods. Go to the house of the old woman in the woods. She will be alone, spinning thread, with a light on in the window. Go inside.

3. The girl receives an item that will change her fortune.

To escape the place that's hurting you, all you need is:
- A kind old woman with gifts
- A way around the monsters who wish to devour you
- A kimono and candy for the theater

When the oni come, the girl spreads rice around her mouth, as though she's died and worms already crawl throughout her flesh.

4. The girl marries a lord.

Clean the house from top to bottom. Give candy to your stepsister when a rich lord is looking. Compose a song of salt and pine and snow. Watch as your stepmother sends her daughter down the hill, unaware of the rocks that line the ground ahead.

Spend no more time mourning your stepsister than you would a broken dish.

The Magical Helper

The woman in the cottage:
gnarled hands spinning
yellow flax.

She will either bless
or curse.

These are the simple facts of life.

A bag, its seam torn:
chestnuts spill out, revealing
the trail that leads home.

The Ordinary Helpers

The woman at the theater:
careful hands clasped within
those of friends

who came to her side with rags
and brooms.

These are the simple facts of life.

The blessing
that is not written down
but only felt.

The Persecuted Heroine (German)

1. A girl is abused by her family.

The demands never cease: dresses spun from silk, invitations to every party, a soft bed at night. She's never seen hunger like that in her sisters' eyes.

2. The girl seeks magical assistance.

There will be a feast at the ball, something more than lentils and breadcrumbs. When she stares long enough into the cinders, she can almost see the table piled high with decadent sweets. Her mouth waters constantly.

3. The girl receives an item that will change her fortune.

To escape the place that's hurting you, all you need is:
- The help of pigeons and turtledoves
- A magic hazel tree
- A dress of silver and gold

At the ball, she eats everything she can get her hands on. When she loses a shoe, it seems a fair trade, the universe demanding payment for her hunger.

She throws the remaining slipper over the fence.

4. The girl marries a prince.

Hundreds of citizens attend the wedding. The guests are served bread and apples, wine and gingerbread, snakeskin and mooncakes. The girl eats until she aches, but still her mouth waters for more.

Lentils

A spell to get to the ball:
remove a bowlful of lentils from the fireplace
and pray your stepmother wasn't lying.

The good ones into the pot,
The bad ones into the crop,

The enduring power of false hope
in a home that can only be escaped
in one of two ways.

Last night, when you stood
over your stepmother's bed,
cleaver in hand, staring down at her.

Or this:

Somewhere on a ballroom floor
is a man as desperate as yourself
if you can reach him.

The good ones into the pot,
The bad ones into the crop,
None into your own stomach.

Sprinkle with hazel ash and carrion feather
and walk in a clockwise circle
three times
around
the house.

The Bloody Shoe

The crumbling manor of her mother's death
is already falling behind them in the woods.

The girl's arms tight around the prince's waist,
her foot within the golden slipper wet
with sweat and other people's blood.

The first night at the ball,
his arms had been around her waist instead,
the subtle smell of cinnamon on his neck

taking all of her strength not to lean in
and lay her tongue against it for a taste.

At the palace, her slippers slide
on marble stairs as the smell of burnt sugar
wafts in from the kitchen.

It is not dinner yet, but she can wait
for the promise of something that burns so sweetly
even as it crumbles to ashes on her tongue.

THE
HEART'S
TRAP

The Maiden and the Beast

1. A father steals a rose to bring home to his daughter.

Where all his other children demanded riches, she asked for a rose, symbolizing—what was it? Life? Death? Innocence? Sex? Or just a flash of color in the heat of summer? He supposes it doesn't matter. It's the thought behind the gift that counts.

2. The beast that owns the garden demands the daughter as payment.

This is what comes of wanting things. There are rules for women's hunger.

3. The girl is permitted a visit home. She overstays the allotted time.

After the luxury of the beast's palace, her home is tight against her skin. Everywhere she moves the maiden brushes up against a sister, an empty cupboard, or a promise she once made. She bathes in a wooden tub with her knees against her chest and ignores the bits of skin that drift away.

She stays a second week.

4. She finds the monster almost dead, and embraces his body.
He becomes a prince.

When she returns to the palace, the monster is lying on the lawn. His scales have gone dull and dusty, his horns broken off at the tips, but worst of all is the gray trickle of blood protruding from his chest. She does not recognize what she is feeling, so it must be love.

After they marry, the maiden covers all the mirrors in the house, frightened that if she glances into one, it will not be her own face looking back.

The Thorn

A maiden in a castle's haunted walls.
Her footsteps make no noise against the dust.
The beast moves slowly, shuffles, drags his claws.

She still can see the fear in Father's eyes
when she agreed to take his punishment.
(Good girl, your father is so much obliged.)

And every evening in the dining room,
the monster offers her a marble ring
and she begs for a final visit home.

The beast relents. At home, the maiden sees
a father with dark circles 'round his eyes.
They fill with tears when she says, "Just a week."

Her sisters come with suckling pig and wine.
They dance. Men's fingers brush against her skin.
As days roll by, she loses track of time.

Until one night she dreams of matted fur
wrapped up in water, drowning in the moat.
She wakes, and to the castle she returns.

His body lies there, swollen, on the grass.
She falls upon her knees, begs him to live,
and promises she'll marry him at last.

The beast leaps to his feet. He starts to change.
His horns fall out. His fur comes off in clumps.
He goes to tell the servants they're engaged.

Left in the garden, she picks up a rose.
Its thorn stabs quickly, leaving her to wince.
(She hadn't guessed the beast would be a prince.)
She blinks—just once—and it has decomposed.

Promise

From across the market, eyes of men
follow the girl selling flowers.
They drive their teeth into rosy apples
and declare them almost ripe.

She tries not to notice
the drops of blood in their palms
as they carry away her roses
like trophies won in war.

But at night when she's alone
splotches of red dance behind her eyes.
She wanders out to her garden, shears in hand.
Come morning, she smiles

at their stems, now dripping and toothless;
a pile of thorns in the dirt at her feet.

Restored to Life

1. A soldier and a princess are wed, vowing to be buried together when one dies.

At the wedding feast, they eat their fill of meats and wines, pushing their bodies to the limit. When they kiss, the rest of the world dissolves. Death is an invisible guest, hiding in the princess's smile and in the curves of her stomach.

Months later, they kiss for the last time. The princess dies with empty eyes and hands.

2. In the tomb, the soldier resurrects the princess.

When their hands have properly bruised against the stone, they are released from the tomb. Citizens from throughout the kingdom come to witness this miracle. The princess's hand trembles in the soldier's, and when no one is looking, she pulls it away.

On the rare occasion that they kiss, her lips are waxy and cold.

3. The princess kills the soldier.

His body sinks into the ocean. That night, for the first time since her death, the princess sleeps.

4. The soldier is resurrected and has the princess drowned.

Her body has been left for the hagfish, but the original tomb still stands where it always did. Some days, the soldier wanders through it, listening to the echo of his own footsteps. The floor is littered with rose petals and empty snakeskins.

The Vow

A soldier weds a princess with the deal
that when one dies, the other will be placed
inside the tomb. Their last breath in that space
will weld their love in death to tempered steel.
The princess sickens and is dead too soon.
The soldier watches flies drift past her head.
This wasn't what he'd meant by "marital bed."
His lover's body soon will be consumed.
A snake slips in the cracks. The soldier breathes,
steps forward, lifts his sword, and stabs it thrice.
Another comes and brings it back to life
with magic plants. The soldier puts these leaves
against the bloodstained lips of his late wife,
and in an instant she gasps back to life.

In death, her love fled from her beatless heart.
Now on a trip together through the sea
their kisses linger most unpleasantly.
She meets the captain. A new romance starts.
Her husband hears their moans and pleasured sighs.
The sea-struck lovers scheme. They make a plan
to throw the husband from the boat. He lands
within the sea's dark clutches, where he dies.
His servant finds him, uses the snake-leaves.
They row home quickly to inform the king.
Hearing his daughter's crimes, the sovereign brings
swift justice. She is drowned. The soldier grieves.
Her few remains rest in a simple grave.
Here lies the princess magic couldn't save.

Marital Bed

The first sensation is a sting
in her left shoulder, movement of some
creeping creature—worms?

Skin slips from her bones.

She takes a sharp breath and begins to count:
the sound of a fly inches from her face,
three ants between her fingers.

Then, eyes peeling open:
a beetle, a sword, a handful of leaves,
a white snake, and

a flash of yellow in her husband's eyes.

The Danced-Out Shoes

1. Twelve princesses leave their palace at night.

Sometimes, the youngest daughter wonders if they should let themselves be caught. But every night, she is gifted with fresh sea air that prickles only of salt and not her father's gaze. Every morning, she awakens with a smile.

> *2. The king sends spies to find out where his daughters have been going.*

In the daytime, he watches their steps closely. The princesses' dirty shoes leave scuff marks on his clean floors. This is not what it means to be king. These were not the rules.

> *3. A soldier follows the princesses to an underground lake.*

As the soldier ignores the drip-drips of the secret tunnel, he keeps his eyes trained on the girls. The youngest seems to know too much and asks too many questions. She does not follow the rules of his story. Beneath the crescent moon, he cannot tell the other girls apart.

> *4. For uncovering the truth, the soldier is permitted to marry the eldest daughter.*

Some mornings, there are holes in her shoes. He tears apart the room, looking for entrances and exits but finds none. The door is kept locked, the key clenched in his fist, and still her shoes fall apart.

He makes a valiant effort not to notice.

Moonlit Fragments

At break of dawn, the king looks for the shoes
and bites his lip. At some point in the night
the soles have shred to bits. The princesses
are sleeping in their beds; see, there they lie.
Their door locks from outside. Still, the soles
of golden slippers have been worn apart.

Each night, he guards their door and falls apart.
Each morning it's the same damn broken shoes.
A trade is offered: if for three full nights
men from the kingdom watch the princesses
the one who can unravel the girls' lie
may wed which one he chooses. He'll be sole

heir to the throne. And if he fails, his soul
will be wrenched out, his body cut apart.
Each man who tries is thwarted, and the shoes
wear through, until a soldier comes one night.
He droops until the wily princesses
think him asleep. When they no longer lie,

he follows down a hidden stair. Fates lie
within his hands, but of the women's souls
the youngest one in fear is set apart.
She hears the thumping of the soldier's shoes
against the forest floor. But through the night,
he stays within sight of the princesses.

Laughter cries out when soon the princesses
approach a gleaming shore where princes lie
in wait. They cross the lake with grins. Their sole
delight begins when they are pulled apart
to dance upon the rocky beach. Their shoes
unravel as they dance into the night.

The soldier follows them the next two nights,
and then informs the king the princesses
go dancing at a lake. He shares their lie.
The secret door is boarded up. The soldier
chooses the eldest girl to set apart.
His wedding robes are dark red like his shoes.

The bride is given glass shoes for her wedding night.
Princesses dance in a frenzied circle until the eldest collapses. She lies
upon the floor, her soles shattered and her feet torn apart.

Shred to Bits

One summer night, she dreams
herself back to the banks of the water,
waltzing lightly in the arms
of a faceless prince.

She awakens in the dark,
her husband's arms wrapped
around her waist, holding her close.
His breath is hot against her neck.

Skin burnt, she slithers out from his arms,
drags her shoes out from under the bed,
begins to spin,

and the moths abandon the moonlight
to join the princess in her frenzied dance.

The Maiden-Killer

1. A husband goes on a journey, telling his young wife not
   to look in the hall closet.

"Don't look," she whispers to herself every night, the words just loud enough to echo in the empty bed chamber. She tells herself she does not want to know. Flies move in lazy circles around the house.

2. The girl opens the closet and finds the bodies of
   her husband's former wives.

Propped against the walls and littering the floor, stacked neatly in cases— there are many ways to display a corpse. The girl looks around her, certain the door has closed her in, but it hangs open. She runs to bed and buries herself beneath the covers.

The flies have vanished from the house. The minutes tick by like drops of blood on stone.

3. The husband returns and threatens to kill her.

The girl marries the monster, and a monster he remains.

4. Her brother arrives and kills the husband.

In stories such as these, there's punishments for evil: a beast's stomach filled with stones, a dance in red-hot shoes, eyes plucked out by ravens. The ending is a happy one.

The girl and her brother try to remove the bodies from the closet and give them a proper burial, but they can't break down the door and the key has gone missing.

The Forbidden Room

A girl walks down the aisle in a white dress.
Her husband-to-be watches her from the altar,
his beard a blue stain against milky skin.
He has six past wives, all dead.

He watches her from the altar.
She shivers at the thought of kissing him.
He has six past wives, all dead, but
she'll be safe as long as she stays out of the hall closet.

She shivers every time she kisses him.
He leaves for a journey and tells her
she'll be safe as long as she stays out of the hall closet.
He gives her keys to all the house's rooms.

He leaves for a journey and tells her
to be a good girl and listen.
He gives her keys to all the house's rooms.
She promises not to look in the closet, but

to be a good girl and listen
will not keep her safe.
She promised not to look in this closet, but
whatever is inside calls out to her.

It will not keep her safe.
She swiftly unlocks the door.
The bodies inside call out to her.
It's full of corpses of past murdered wives.

She swiftly slams the door.
When she closes her eyes, she can
still see the corpses of past murdered wives.
The key is stained with blood.

When she closes her eyes, she can
pretend that it is clean. It won't wash off.
The key is stained with blood.
She hides it beneath a floorboard,

pretends that it is clean. It won't wash off.
At night she hears it dripping on the stone
where she's hidden it beneath a floorboard.
When her husband returns, he asks for it.

That night, she hears blood dripping against stone.
Her brother had promised to visit her today.
Her husband comes, asks for the key again.
She watches out the window.

(She is sure her brother had promised to visit today.)
She asks for time to pray, but plans to stall
and watch out the window.
Her husband agrees. He'll kill her soon enough.

He gives her a few hours to pray. She stalls.
At last, there are sails upon the horizon.
Her husband will be here to kill her soon.
She chokes on every single breath she takes,

but at last! Sails on the horizon.
The door slams open.
She chokes on every breath she takes.
A sword gleams in his hand.

The door lies open.
The girl shrieks, but sees her brother.
The sword gleams in his hand
as it plunges through her husband's ribs.

She shrieks and runs to her brother.
The blood spills out onto the floor,
a sword plunged through her husband's ribs.
His face, in death, forming a sickly grin.

The blood spills out onto the floor,
leaving a blue stain on his milky skin.
His face, in death, has formed a sickly grin.
The girl walks down the aisle in a black dress.

Stained

She can smell the bodies—
like fertilizer, like when she used to bury
seeds, back when she had a garden
and knew how to make things grow.

Still in pigtails and short dresses, nails
caked in mud, and out of breath
from running from her brothers.

The worms between the dirt clods had been pink.

There are worms here too.
Small and white, they writhe.
She prays she'll soon wake up.

Nails dug into her own palms, blood
dripping onto the key, and the bodies
still carefully displayed, broken
like the tender stems of daisies

as they were snapped between her brothers' fingers.

The Entombed Princess

1. A princess is locked in a tower for seven years for wishing to choose her husband.

Her hair grows long over time. It knots and tangles around her shoulders, and she never bothers to comb it straight. Once, four years in, she tries to hack it off. The bread knife snags in her curls, refusing to sever them.

2. When she gets out, the man she'd hoped to marry is betrothed.

When she glimpses him, all she can see is the solidity of his body. This is a man who has never had to soak rice in tepid water and eat it raw. He has never counted a barrel of almonds three times over, praying for more than were there in the morning. He is beautiful and well.

Some nights, she dreams that he is sitting in a barrel of water. Sometimes, she reaches for his head and holds him under until the bubbles stop.

3. The true bride asks the princess to take her place.

The chapel was built from the same gray stones as her tower. The air is stale and full of dust. The princess holds tightly to her veil, refusing to take it off even when the man leans in for a kiss.

ATU 870

4. This comes to light, and the true bride's head is chopped off.

The princess closes her eyes, but the smell of hot metal makes her vomit. When it is over, she forces herself to look at her husband, unsure of who she will see.

He is the same man that he always was.

They remain in love, and live happily ever after.

Urtica Dioica

When after seven years no one has saved her from the tower,
the princess takes a bread knife in her hands and begins to chip away
at the mortar until the stones tumble to the ground and she is free.

A ragged princess in the countryside
escapes the rubble of her former land.
She lives off nettles and old donkey hide.

She walks until she cannot bear to stand,
then begs for work in the kingdom of
a prince who once had pleaded for her hand.

Her heart, though raw, beats with forbidden love.
The prince, in three days' time, is set to wed
a woman, shrouded by her veil and gloves.

But on that day the true bride hides her head.
"I am too ugly, can't be seen," she cries.
She veils the princess, sends her out instead.

The princess steels herself, but cannot lie.
She whispers to the church at her approach,
"Church-door, break not, but I am no true bride."

She speaks the wedding vows, her heart afloat.
The veil kept tightly closed around her face.
A precious chain is placed around her throat.

That evening, the time comes for their embrace.
The true bride climbs into the prince's bed
The prince raises the veil to see her face

and knows at once she's not the one he wed.
He sends out men to find the other bride.
The true bride tells them, "Chop off that girl's head."

But when the prince lays eyes on her, he cries.
He knows at once that she's his former love.
The axe is dropped. His head falls to her thighs.

The false bride, who is watching from above,
is killed. The stone is spattered with her blood.

The True Bride

Even after the end of the story—
when she lies in his arms, whispers drifting
across her skin, "safe, safe,"

she dreams of stone walls coming closer,
cutting off her airways as beetles climb through
dark cracks in the walls.

She wonders if she could fit through those holes.

The prince snores in their bed, untroubled
by the stain in the courtyard that no one
has been able to scrub out.

It's harder to forget than she'd expected.

In the morning, she stares at her reflection,
where a new growth of nettles has emerged
in the places where the bread knife
sawed through hair.

INTERLUDE
TWO

The Persecuted Heroine (Iranian)

1. A girl is abused by her family.

The demands never cease: spin the cotton, sort it into piles, kill your mother and choose your father's new wife, don't let the yellow cow out of the vinegar jar.

You'd think the girl never learned the word "no."

2. The girl seeks magical assistance.

There is a demon in the well who will lie to you and a yellow cow who will tell you the truth. There is good in the world. There is harm in the world. They live inside the same stone enclosure.

3. The girl receives an item that will change her fortune.

To escape the place that's hurting you, all you need is:
- A yellow cow
- To disobey the orders of a Dīv
- A friendly wind

(But she lies and gives the wrong instructions to her stepsister. The girl is rewarded, her stepsister punished, and all comes to a happy end.)

4. The girl marries a prince.

Separate the beans from the lentils. Cry until you've filled a jar with tears. Put on these beautiful clothes and go. Get in the oven, so the prince won't test the shoe upon your foot. Cover up the moon on your forehead and the bright star on your chin.

Or don't.

The Outgrowing of a Mother

Count the vinegar jars.
Count them twice
until you reach the seventh, then
unscrew the lid   and throw your mother in.

Sprinkle coriander in your hair
and let it fall   into the fireplace.
Make sure your father sees.
Tell him you need   a mother
to keep it clean.

Hang a liver   on the door.
Tell your father to marry   the woman
who first knocks her head
against it.

Lie in front of the fire all night
weeping   weeping
for the dead   mother
weeping for yourself,
weeping because you did
as you were told.

Contrary, Backwards, Inside Out

Kill your mother, says the mulla.
Yes, says the girl.
Make me your father's new wife.
Yes, says the girl.
Spin the pile of cotton.
Yes, says the girl.
Don't let it fall into the well.

But the cotton falls into the well.

Go into the well, says the yellow cow.
Yes, says the girl.
Salam the dīv nicely.
Yes, says the girl.
Find the wisp of cotton.
Yes, says the girl.
Come back home to me.

The girl goes into the well.

Come break my head, says the dīv.
No, says the girl, and washes her hair.
Break the water jars.
No, says the girl, and fills them.
Knock down my house.
No, says the girl, and sweeps it.
Take whatever treasure you desire.

And she does.

The Persecuted Heroine (Russian)

1. A girl is abused by her family.

The demands never cease: chop wood, work the fields, do the dishes, go into the woods and bring back a coal for the hearth. What food she's given, the girl feeds to her doll. She isn't very hungry anymore.

But the fire still needs its fuel.

2. The girl seeks magical assistance.

Go to the woods. Go to the house of the witch in the woods. Walk past her skeleton gate, pulling the jawbone latch aside so you may enter. But first you must follow the chicken-step footprints through the dark forest to her clearing. She will not do you the courtesy of waiting in one place.

3. The girl receives an item that will change her fortune.

To escape the place that's hurting you, all you need to do is:
   o Separate the mildewed ears of corn
   o Separate the poppy seeds from the dirt
   o Remember to feed the magic doll

When the witch sees that the girl is blessed, she gifts her a fiery skull and sends her home.

The girl shuts the jawbone latch and breaks into a run.

ATU 510A

4. The girl marries a king.

The fire burns down her home with her family inside, and the girl moves to the city. She weaves so beautifully that she is soon discovered by a king, as must happen to girls in these tales.

At the wedding feast, the girl slips a taste of everything to the doll in her pocket: lentils and mooncakes, poppyseed muffins, and the last crumbs of her bread.

Poppyseeds

Consider this:
A girl, standing underneath
a full moon
bony fingers in pockets caressing

the soft shells of worn-out
breadcrumbs: a spell
to cast to find her way home safely—
or, consider this instead:

A girl is nothing
so much as a warm meal,
cornbread that melts on the
tip of your tongue—
A girl is nothing.

Mere electricity
and the subtleties of moonlight.

Cinders

A girl walks home alone at night,
  with a flaming skull clasped tightly in her palms.
No wolves lurking in the backdrop this time.

Home is through the forest
  and closer than she thought.

She can see her sisters — look!
  They are mere shadows on the doorstep
    that drop their weaving and run forward,
  arms outstretched

  but not for her.
    It is the fire they need,
in the deep ice of winter.
  The doll inside her pocket wants to scream.

  But the skull precedes the scream.
Shiny embers leaping toward the hearth, then
  the place where the hearth is not.
    Far too brash and angry, like her heart.

  She watches it burn, her own teeth
tearing against the skin of her cheeks, and
  the blood
  the blood trickles down her throat
    like boiling milk.

THE
JOURNEY
HOME

The Animal Bridegroom

1. A girl is married to an animal.

Her father asks. Her father asks. Her father asks. There is a reason she must do this and that is for her family. If it can be called a choice, then it is hers.

This is not the story you think it is. There are glimmers of sameness; pebbles that in the dark look quite a lot like breadcrumbs. They are dangerous, yes, but oh so smooth against the tongue.

2. The animal becomes a man.

Three drops of tallow on a white shirt. A bearskin rug. A beast who was only ever a man, and that is the truth, forever and ever, amen.

3. The man is taken far away.

There is no road to the castle where he's been taken. The girl will never find her way, and they tell her this. Perhaps she will go home. Perhaps she will return to a father who asks, and asks, and asks. Perhaps.

4. The girl goes on a journey to rescue him.

He is only human now, but that is all right. She forgives him the soft skin where there once was fur; forgives the bones she feels when he squeezes her hand. Sometimes, when he throws the bearskin rug over his lap, she lays her head upon it and remembers.

As the nights grow warm, the rug is put away.

Carried by the Wind

His soft fur always made her wince,
but in the dark he seemed a prince.
She lit a match to see his face.
She has not seen her husband since.

Hands clutching her torn wedding lace,
she wanders through the woods and lakes.
She finds a stooped old woman—witch?—
who looks at her with mild distaste.

The girl's eyes drop. Her fingers twitch.
The crone speaks in a droning pitch.
"East of the sun, west of the moon."
She gives the girl a horse and gift.

The girl rides through the frigid air,
thinks of the curse she'd set astir.
When her eyes droop, she dreams about
her marriage to the polar bear.

"East of the sun, west of the moon."
The next two witches also croon.
They send her to seek out the wind.
She wanders deserts and lagoons.

Her husband, kidnapped for her sins.
Is it too late to rescue him?
She climbs the mountains with a prayer.
She finds the Houses of the Winds.

The maiden begs to travel where
her love had gone to disappear.
The north wind says he'll take her there.
But after that, it's up to her.

Seek Out the Wind

The polar bear said, "Are you frightened?"
No, she wasn't.

There was no road to the castle.
"You'll get there either too late or never at all."
Yes, that could very well be true.

He was so wild and furious.
"I once blew an aspen leaf there . . .
. . . if you're not afraid to go with me."

She was not afraid, no matter what bad things might happen.

They went far,
so far that no one would believe
how far they went.

"Are you frightened?" said the North Wind.
"No," she said, she wasn't.

The Magic Flight

1. Three princesses are raised by a witch.

She teaches them the art of what she does. She lifts their chins and tells them to hold their heads up high. They dress in black but do not fly on broomsticks. In the evenings, when their hands are clasped together so hard that barbed-wire marks appear, the universe whispers, "Alive, alive, alive."

2. A prince comes to visit.

Between one place and another there is a palace he has never seen before. The women inside are strange and beautiful. The sun leaves the sky in stained-glass ridges: golden, red, and pink.

3. The witch tries to kill him.

Her upturned lips, rimmed with red. Three drops of something in his wine. A knife hidden in her pocket. The two older sisters stand tall, chins up high, wearing black crepe that goes up beyond their necks. The youngest shakes and droops, a willow among oaks. She is not ready. Alive. A-live. A life.

4. The youngest princess saves him.

They run away. She kills the witch. She lives her life.

The Witch Dies *A Triptych*

... in the stories of princesses, we see the ways in which women attempt to take control of their own lives. For example, Morgan Le Fay studies with the sorcerer Merlin as a way to take back agency after Uther Pendragon... however, Pendragon is lauded as a great king, Morgan as a mere witch. In the Grimm stories, Snow White runs away from a wicked (step)mother... with regards to these tales, it is important to take a wider view and also examine the role of the prince, discussed on page... as Marina Warner points out, the voice of the male speaker often disguises itself as the benign figure of Mother Goose... The ladies of the lake provide another example... girlhood can only exist in these two modes. The folklore hero has his sword, while... witchcraft provides the one alternative...The heroine either swallows her feelings or is consumed by them... the woman who stabs does so with a needle. In what ways do we come to understand the folklore heroine... in counterpoint, I do feel compelled to point out that many folktales have yet to be discovered by English readers, and may provide...

                    princess

        studies with

                                                                great
                    witch   runs
away   with
                                                        the prince

            disguises   self as
                    lake   girl
                                        has   sword
        witch
swallows her   consumed   woman   stabs
                    way

                                                        out

Princess studies
with great witch.
Runs away

with the prince.
Disguises self as lake.
Girl has sword.

Witch swallows her.
Consumed woman
stabs way out.

Stabs Way Out

A reverse Caesarian: a daughter
who escapes her mother through
the sharp end of a blade

and the space it leaves behind.

One-Eye, Two-Eyes, and Three-Eyes

1. A maiden is starved by her mother.

Her older sister has only one eye, in the center of her forehead. The youngest sister has three. We do not know how many eyes the mother has, only that they are always watching.

2. Her mother kills the goat that gives her food.

She'd like to say it was a friend, but what she misses most is the feeling of a full belly. Her sisters offer her their crusts of bread, but she refuses, terrified her mother may be looking.

3. The maiden plants the goat's entrails and a magic tree grows.

It's not a way out, but on cold nights she climbs to the top of the tree until her entire body feels as though it's been frozen. Her heart slows until she can barely hear it over the whipping of the air. She bites the fruit, its gold skin giving way to something sweet.

In the distance, she can see houses that belong to other, kinder people.

4. A knight offers to take the maiden away with him in exchange for a fruit from the tree.

When she says yes, the tree lowers several branches just for him.

The Tree

A maiden, plagued with hunger, sits out in the field one hot summer.
A crone wanders by the dry well and offers this girl a goat spell.
"Bleat, my little goat, bleat. Cover the table with something to eat.
Bleat, bleat, my little goat, I pray, and take the table quite away."

She no longer begs for her supper. Suspicion grows inside her mother.
Her sisters follow her as spies. The youngest uses her third eye.
Their mother, anger in her throat, slits the neck of the nanny goat.
Bleat, bleat, my little goat, I pray. They took the table quite away.

The girl buries in earth the goat's liver. Up grows a tree of gold and silver
with apples growing, fresh and sweet. Her sisters beg for some to eat.
They reach for it with grasping hands. She whispers in a soft command,
"Bleat, bleat, my little goat, I pray, and take your branches quite away."

A knight admires the silver tree, says, "Pluck the fruit and come with me."
"Take me away," the maiden pleads, "and I will share my magic tree."
Her mother reaches for her arm. The maiden steals herself from harm.
"Bleat, bleat, my little goat, I pray, and take me from here right away."

A Goat Spell

Step One:
Collect the entrails
of your favorite animal.

Refuse to eat them, even when your stomach
rumbles and you know they would serve well enough as food.

Step Two:
Bury them deep beneath the dirt
all because a woman you don't know
told you it would keep you safe.

As the meat begins to disappear beneath so much dirt,
all you can think about is what you'll be given for breakfast.

Step Three:
Let the image of what will grow
appear inside your mind.

Your sister's rejected bread crusts, maybe,
or oatmeal burned to the bottom of the pan, but
that's not what you imagine.

Instead, you picture something golden, something so ripe
that when you bite into it, juice will spill down your fingers
like something almost real.

Rescue by the Sister

1. A troll kidnaps three sisters, killing two.

As is the case in these stories, refusal to answer the call means death. The girl will not refuse. She will live in the mountain surrounded by rubies and the corpses of those who came before. She will eat the flesh of goats that stumble their way through the same trap door that undid her. She will smile at the troll and close her eyes when she kisses him.

And when he's out of the house, she'll rifle through the rooms until there's something she can use.

2. The youngest revives the others and sends them home.

Reward for being the eldest sister: first to die, and first to live. She's carried by the very troll who killed her, surrounded in her sack by gold and food. He will not see her or the treasure, but a hole in the sack will leave a trail of golden pebbles in her wake.

3. She escapes.

Reward for being the youngest sister: cunning, intelligence, and courage. She leaves not through a sack but out the front door when the troll is away. Her shirt is stained with ruby drops of sweat. She will live. She will be her own sweetheart.

She will never follow a hen into the mountain again.

ATU 311

4. The troll searches for her until sunrise kills him.

He's still frozen somewhere in the woods, but you won't find him. Even the hen never returned from the forest. Only the mountain is still there, rocky boulders casting shadows that hide all that's underneath.

The Sweetheart

"Go looking for your sisters." They'd been caught.
The girl goes off to find them, heart in knots.
That night she falls into the hole
of a small tearstained mountain troll.
She kisses him, pretends she's merely lost.

That night she lies awake in his cold cot.
Her sisters are entombed here, caked in rot.
How can she make their broken bodies whole?
Go looking.

A potion in a tarnished copper pot,
and back to life the sisters have been brought.
They run away with pockets full
and sunlight kills the weeping troll.
Where is the place where his life came to naught?
Go looking.

That Night

Those vile nights — the waiting,
the interminable
tapping of rain on a roof

tap tock tick tap

She sits across from
the sweetheart who smiles
with boulders for teeth

and who would break her spine
if he knew how much time she spent
in the drip-drip cellar

where her dead sisters lie.

Keeper of the Dwarves

1. A queen orders her daughter be killed.

A mirror shows the truth, but flipped. The girl never asked to be beautiful, never asked for anything except a warm bed and enough food to eat. She is only a child. She has not yet learned how to long for things.

2. The assassin takes pity and abandons the girl in the woods.

Golden light streams through the trees, but an owl hoots in the distance. She has very little time. There is nothing inviting about this cottage, no gingerbread panels or sugar-spun glass, but there is a bed. Her feet dangle from the end, and in moments, she's asleep.

3. The queen finds out the girl is alive and poisons her.

There are safe paths through the forest. The dwarves warn her of things not from the woods: wolves who eat children and strange men who make dangerous deals. She listens but does not understand, in the way that children refuse to believe in monsters even when they meet one in their dreams.

When she bites into the apple, it is crisp and sweet.

ATU 709

4. A prince saves the girl, and they are married soon after.

The path to the castle wakes the girl, forces the rotting fruit from her throat. She returns to life to tell him no, to refuse the sort of home that poisons young girls, locks them in towers, forces them to spin straw into gold or leaves them in the woods. She will not return to a castle, even his.

They remain in the forest, king and queen of their own little cottage. They live happily ever after.

The Fairest One of All

"Oh tell me, ugly mirror on the wall,"
the queen demands, sitting atop her throne.
"Who in this land is fairest of us all?"
She sits and waits. The answer is well-known,
the only name she ever hears her own.
The mirror flashes, fills the room with light.
The queen goes faint. She stumbles and she moans,
sure what the mirror said cannot be right:
"Your daughter is more beautiful tonight."

The queen screams for her hunter. He appears.
She strokes his face and whispers, "Take the girl
into the forest. Fill her heart with fear,
then cut it out." He bows. His knuckles curl.
Out in the woods, he grabs the girl and snarls
that if she wants to live, then she must run.
Her bare feet soon are torn apart by burs.
She stumbles on a house, and falls down stunned.
The dwarves that own it let her in at once.

And when the dwarves go out for work each day,
they warn her of the dangers in the land.
It disappoints her that she cannot stray
with all the pleasures of the woods at hand.
She sits at home and views the meadowland.
Far off, a mirror's propped upon a shelf.
It speaks the truth at the foul queen's demand:
her daughter's being kept alive in stealth.
Her eyes slam shut. She'll kill the girl herself.

The queen, disguised, looks like a tired old hag.
She offers up an apple, bright and red.
The young girl savors it as her teeth drag
across the skin. Then she collapses, dead.
The dwarves find her prone body, shake their heads,
and place her in a coffin built from glass.
A man arrives, a crown around his head.
He lifts her out and sets her on the grass.
The fruit is jostled from her throat. She gasps.

The maiden wakes, stuck with wild vengeance.
How best to punish? Her eyes flash with red.
She'll find her mother and force her to dance
in hot iron shoes until she meets her end.
She asks the dwarves what they would recommend.
What punishment could suit the woman who
would poison her own daughter, leave her dead?
But what they say, it rings to her as true.
"Revenge may hurt her, but it will destroy you."

The dwarves suggest the queen can keep her throne.
The girl, instead, will abdicate her right.
The forest will not be a place of fright,
and here she'll build a life that is her own.

A Life That is Her Own

And after the end of the story—
when he's kissed her, and she's awake,
and the birds and deer cry out, "safe, safe,"

she makes herself a home inside the woods.
A cottage at the edge of a meadow
with a winding path that leads away
toward dark places she has never been.

She feels no need to follow it.

There is no sugar-spun façade, no wolf
lying in wait, no glass coffin,
only moss-covered wood
and the redeeming light

that spills in through the cracks of the sky.

The prince has traded in his crown.
The desert to the south is full of the past,
and she doesn't mind.

In the morning, she glances at her reflection,
where a coronet of vines has begun to form
against the ripples
of her hair.

SOURCE MATERIAL

Like most lovers of fairy tales, I believe there is no one true version of any of these stories. For the purposes of this volume, I chose one form as my focus for each tale-type listed. While I weave other variants into the manuscript, this list consists of the stories I relied on most heavily.

ATU 306 (page 63): "The Shoes That Were Danced to Pieces," from *Grimm's Complete Fairy Tales* (Barnes & Noble Books, 1993). Based on the Grimms' 1857 manuscript, translator unstated.

ATU 310 (page 30): "Rapunzel," from *Grimm's Complete Fairy Tales* (Barnes & Noble Books, 1993). Based on the Grimms' 1857 manuscript, translator unstated.

ATU 311 (page 106): "The Three Sisters Who Were Taken Into the Mountain," collected by Peter Christen Asbjørnsen and Jørgen Moe. Translated by Tiina Nunnally in *The Complete and Original Norwegian Folktales of Asbjørnsen and Moe* (2019).

ATU 312 (page 67): "Bluebeard," translated from Charles Perrault in Andrew Lang's *Blue Fairy Book* (1889).

ATU 313 (page 98): "Outwitting the Witch," collected by Franz Xaver von Schönwerth. Translated by Shelley Tanaka in *White as Milk, Red as Blood: The Forgotten Fairy Tales of Franz Xaver von Schönwerth* (2018).

ATU 327A (page 19): "Hansel and Gretel," translated by D. L. Ashliman from the Grimm's 1812 manuscript.

ATU 333 (page 35): "Little Riding Hood," from *Grimm's Complete Fairy Tales* (Barnes & Noble Books, 1993). Based on the Grimms' 1857 manuscript, translator unstated.

ATU 410 (page 22): "The Sleeping Beauty," from *Grimm's Complete Fairy Tales* (Barnes & Noble Books, 1993). Based on the Grimms' 1857 manuscript, translator unstated.

ATU 425A (page 93): "East of the Sun and West of the Moon," collected by Peter Christen Asbjørnsen and Jørgen Moe. Translated by Tiina Nunnally in *The Complete and Original Norwegian Folktales of Asbjørnsen and Moe* (2019).

ATU 425C (page 53): "Beauty and the Beast," from *The Provensen Book of Fairy Tales* (1971). Based off of Jeanne-Marie Leprince de Beaumont's version, translator unstated.

ATU 500 (page 26): "Rumpelstiltskin," from *Grimm's Complete Fairy Tales* (Barnes & Noble Books, 1993). Based on the Grimms' 1857 manuscript, translator unstated.

ATU 510A (page 41): "Benizara and Kakezara," collected by Keigo Seki. Translated by Robert J. Adams.

ATU 510A (page 45): "Cinderella," translated by D. L. Ashliman from the Grimms' 1857 manuscript.

ATU 510A (page 81): "The Story of Little Fatima," collected and translated by D.L.R. Lorimer and E.O. Lorimer.

ATU 510A* (page 86): "Vasilisa the Beautiful," collected by Alexander Afanasyev. Translated by Post Wheeler. It is listed here as 510A* due to scholarly debates as to whether this is the best ATU categorization for this story.

ATU 511 (page 103): "One-Eye, Two-Eyes, and Three-Eyes," from *Grimm's Complete Fairy Tales* (Barnes & Noble Books, 1993). Based on the Grimms' 1857 manuscript, translator unstated.

ATU 612 (page 58): "The Three Snake-Leaves," from *Grimm's Complete Fairy Tales* (Barnes & Noble Books, 1993). Based on the Grimms' 1857 manuscript, translator unstated.

ATU 709 (page 110): "Little Snow White," translated by D. L. Ashliman from the Grimms' 1812 manuscript.

ATU 870 (page 74): "Maid Maleen," from *Grimm's Complete Fairy Tales* (Barnes & Noble Books, 1993). Based on the Grimms' 1857 manuscript, translator unstated.

NOTES

Further Notes on the ATU Index

Like all forms of classification, the ATU system is more subjective than it appears. It was designed by men whose understanding of folklore was informed primarily by European stories. Because of this, some of the delineations that seemed clear to them become problematic when stories from other cultures are brought into consideration. For example, the categories of ATU 333 (which includes Little Red Riding Hood) and ATU 123 (which includes The Wolf and the Kids) are separated because the latter is considered an animal tale. However, the Chinese story of Grandaunt Tiger, classified as ATU 333, contains many motifs of ATU 123. Sociologist Wolfram Eberhard has used this tale to question the distinctions between these tale types. There are also stories such as Vasilisa the Beautiful from Slavic folklore that do not fit neatly into the criteria for any ATU number as currently classified, leading to debates over which category is the most fitting. I highlight these points not to dismiss the system, but as a reminder that it is a human construction that requires constant reworking as our understanding improves.

Page 19, "The Children With The Witch"

For most of the Grimm stories, I made use of the 1857 manuscripts, as they are the most popular and widely-known versions of the stories. I made a few exceptions when I found the 1812 texts more interesting, particularly with regards to the mothers. In between the 1812 and 1819 editions of their book, the Grimm Brothers made the notable change of rewriting many of the less sympathetic mother figures into stepmothers. Hansel and Gretel contains one of these cases. This change remained through the following iterations and is consistent with their final 1857 manuscript.

Page 20, "Sugarcoated"
Hansel and Gretel are only allowed to return home because of the riches they bring with them. Without this change in fortune, their family would still be starving and the children left to continue fending for themselves.

Page 25, "Doesn't Mind at All"
In Giambattista Basile's 1634 story based on this tale type, titled *Sun, Moon, and Talia,* the Sleeping Beauty character is raped by the prince and does not awaken until after giving birth to twins.

Page 26, "The Name"
In the ATU classification system, Rumpelstiltskin stories are listed as ATU 500, "Guessing the Name of the Helper." As Jack Zipes points out in his essay "Spinning with Fate: Rumpelstiltskin and the Decline of Female Productivity," Rumpelstiltskin is as much a blackmailer as he is a helper.

Page 27, "Straw for Gold"
There's an interesting triangulation in Rumpelstiltskin stories. The dwarf (often portrayed using antisemitic stereotypes) is coded as the

villain. The true villainy of the king's ultimatum, in which the heroine must spin straw to gold or be killed, is brushed to the side.

Page 35, "The Glutton"
In the Grimm version, Little Red Cap is rescued. This is not true in every version; notably, Charles Perrault's 1697 manuscript ends in the girl's death and a pithy little moral about why young girls shouldn't talk to strangers.

Page 41, "The Persecuted Heroine (Japanese)"
The source text I used for this piece was "Benizara and Kakezara." Benizara, or "Crimson Dish," is the name of the protagonist, while Kakezara, or "Broken Dish" is the name of the stepsister. Oni are a type of Japanese demon, often associated with ogres or trolls. In 510A tales, one of the key criteria is the "slipper test," in which a key trait is used to determine whether the protagonist or the stepsister is the woman the male character met. In this story, both are asked to compose a poem. The woman who writes a better poem is chosen as the bride.

Page 44, "The Ordinary Helpers"
When reading this story, I was struck by the fact that while there is a magical helper, her assistance does not advance the heroine to the central event, but only provides her with her kimono. Instead, it is the girl's ordinary friends who help her complete the stepmother's tasks in time to make it to the theater.

Page 47, "Lentils"
"The good ones into the pot,/ the bad ones into the crop" is the instruction that the protagonist gives to the birds who assist her in

the stepmother's impossible task. In this case, a pot of lentils has been tossed into the ashes, and the girl must separate them in time for the ball. This language comes from D.L. Ashliman's translation of the 1857 text.

Page 49, "The Bloody Shoe"
The protagonist of this story is only permitted to try on the shoe after her stepsisters have hacked off parts of their feet and left the slipper full of blood.

Page 53, "The Maiden and the Beast"
The best-known version of "Beauty and the Beast" is a pared down version of a 1740 novella. It is not a folktale in the technical sense, but instead a literary fairy tale with folklore roots. It is considered to be a subsect of ATU 425, which includes the myth of Cupid and Psyche.

Page 55, "The Thorn"
In the translation I worked from, the line "Then you are a good girl, and I am very much obliged to you" is spoken by the Beast. I found this strangely haunting. From my earliest conception of Beauty, I saw her as a character who becomes trapped in a "good girl" role so completely that she would rather sacrifice her own life than admit to any iota of selfishness.

Page 58, "Restored to Life"
In the earlier drafts of this book, my close readers almost unilaterally commented that they wanted to know why the princess no longer loves the soldier once she's been brought back to life. This is not explained in the text.

Page 63, "The Danced-Out Shoes"

I find it both fun and peculiar that the princesses are punished for going out dancing with princes, an act that, especially if it leads to a marriage alliance, is often rewarded in European folktales.

Page 73, "Stained"

The brother in Bluebeard is a curiosity. He is at the same time the Deus ex Machina for our heroine, and a reminder that male power is the only way Perrault saw fit to give this story a happy ending.

Page 76, "Urtica Dioica"

One of the things I was most struck by in this story was the seamless transition from "true bride" to "false bride" when referencing the fiancé.

Page 81, "The Persecuted Heroine (Iranian)"

While the heroine's murder of her birth mother is not common in 510A stories, it is also not unique to this specific telling. In fact, there are several examples of this motif cross-culturally. Typically, it occurs on the orders of a teacher or governess who would like to marry the father. In these cases, the teacher becomes the evil stepmother.

Page 84, "Contrary, Backwards, Inside Out"

Reading this story, I was fascinated by the role of the Dīv. One of the criteria of 510A stories is the presence of a magical helper, but usually this character takes the role of a benign figure. The Dīv, on the other hand, is a demon. In my research, I found that Dīv are known for being contrary figures, which may explain why it was important that the protagonist do the opposite of what she is told. At the beginning of the story, the heroine is far too obedient, even killing her mother when her mulla (teacher) instructs her to. By the end, she has learned from the Dīv that there are times when it is important, even life-saving, not to do as told.

Page 86, "The Persecuted Heroine (Russian)"
Here we have another demonic helper: the Baba Yaga. One of my all-time favorite characters, Baba Yaga is a witch from Slavic Folklore. People often go to her for help, but there is always the chance that she'll eat you instead. This story is often classified as 510A, but very loosely. It lacks the important motif of the slipper test, and while the protagonist does marry a king, it is more of an afterthought to the rest of the story.

Page 93, "The Animal Bridegroom"
425A predates 425C by over a millennium but is now the lesser-known of the two. To me, ATU 425A feels like a more fleshed out "Beauty and the Beast," with a proper adventure and a heroine who without a doubt loves the creature she has married.

Page 97, "Seek Out the Wind"
This is a collage poem consisting solely of lines from Tiina Nunnally's wonderful translation of "East of the Sun and West of the Moon," from *The Complete and Original Norwegian Folktales of Asbjørnsen and Moe* (2019). I loved the playful and determined energy of the protagonist.

Page 99, "The Witch Dies"
The article used in this poem is my own invention. The line referring to works not yet translated into English is a reference to the source material for this poem. "Outwitting the Witch" was one of over 500 unpublished folktales by Franz Xaver von Schönwerth discovered in 2012 in an archive in Regensburg. A collection of these stories was

translated into English in 2018. Von Schönwerth was a contemporary of the Grimm Brothers, and therefore provides an interesting counterpoint to their work. In particular, his female characters are of a different sort than most of what we find in Grimm. Even in the same region and time period, there's much more diversity in folklore than we collectively imagine there to be.

Page 102, "Stabs Way Out"
In folklore, witches and mothers often come hand in hand.

Page 103, "One-Eye, Two-Eyes, and Three-Eyes"
For all of the other poems that begin a set, I crafted a title drawn from the ATU index and avoided naming a specific version of the story. However, I could not find an alternate title for ATU 511.

Page 104, "The Tree"
"Bleat, my little goat, bleat. Cover the table with something to eat. / Bleat, bleat, my little goat, I pray, and take the table quite away" comes directly from *Grimm's Complete Fairy Tales* (Barnes & Noble Books, 1993, translator unstated).

Page 110, "Keeper of the Dwarves"
Another example of a mother in the 1812 edition becoming a stepmother by 1857. I chose to stick with the mother in this one as well.

Page 112, "The Fairest One of All"
The ending is my own. In the Grimm version, Snow White marries the prince, takes rule of the kingdom, and forces her mother to dance in red-hot shoes until she drops dead from the pain.

ACKNOWLEDGMENTS

This book began as a capstone project in my final year at Seattle University. I owe a huge debt of gratitude to Mary-Antoinette Smith and Gabriella Gutierrez y Muhs for believing in my work and encouraging me to apply for English Honors. I am also indebted to my mentor Sharon Cumberland, my capstone advisor Charles Tung, and all the other members of my cohort.

This book would not exist without the support of my wife, Elizabeth Nellams, who was willing to sit with me for hours while I ran my thoughts through the brain blender over and over again. Amy Deyerle-Smith bought me fairy tales books for every gift-giving event. Sierra Castor, Jenny Kelson, Ceili Erickson, and Amieka Skeem were all phenomenal trusted readers at various times in the process of this book. I would also like to thank my parents Heath and Cindy Spencer, who have always believed in my writing and in me. I could not have done it without you.

Finally, a special shout-out to my First Matter Press family, who turned this book from an idea to a reality. I felt so held and loved by this community, and am honored to work with such thoughtful and talented people.

Several of these pieces have been published previously in journals or anthologies:

"The Children With The Witch" first appeared in issue 6.2 of *Snapdragon: a Journal of Art and Healing.*

"Breadcrumbs" first appeared in *Bare Bones* (2021) ed. Stephanie Lamb.

"The Sleeping Princess" first appeared in Volume 41, issue 1 of *Plainsongs Magazine.*

"The Name" first appeared in Volume 8 of *The Festival Review.*

"The Maiden in the Tower" first appeared in issue 2 of *Red Ogre Review.*

"The Glutton" first appeared in *Bare Bones* (2021) ed. Stephanie Lamb under the title "Little Red Riding Hood."

"The Wolf" first appeared in Volume 5 of *Sheila-Na-Gig's* Writers Under 30 series.

"A Devouring Too Brief" first appeared in *We Don't Break, We Burn* (2020) ed. Zachary Kluckman.

"The Persecuted Heroine (Japanese)" first appeared in Volume 8 of *The Festival Review.*

"The Maiden-Killer" first appeared in *The Rewritten* (2020) ed. Ruchi Acharya under the title "The Bluebeard."

"The Forbidden Room" first appeared in *Haunted Are These Houses* (2018) ed. Eddie Generous and Erin Sweet Al-Mehairi.

"Stained" first appeared in Issue 42 of *Slipstream.*

"The True Bride" first appeared in *Bare Bones* (2021) ed. Stephanie Lamb.

"The Outgrowing of a Mother" first appeared in Volume 2 of *The Vital Sparks.*

"The Persecuted Heroine (Iranian)" was read aloud on episode 24 of the Mytholadies podcast. It first appeared in print in Volume 8 of *The Festival Review*.

"Poppyseeds" first appeared in *Lore* (2022) ed. Miranda Williams and Nathan Buckingham.

"The Persecuted Heroine (Russian)" was read aloud on episode 24 of the Mytholadies podcast.

"Seek Out the Wind" first appeared in Issue 4 of *Hairstreak Butterfly Review*, under the title "Too Late or Not at All." It is a found language poem, and all lines are drawn directly from Tiina Nunnally's wonderful translation of "East of the Sun and West of the Moon."

"Stabs Way Out" first appeared in volume 116 of *Poet Lore*.

"One-Eye, Two-Eyes, and Three-Eyes" first appeared in Volume 8 of the *Festival Review*.

"A Life That is Her Own" first appeared in Volume 1 of *Sunflowers at Midnight*.

HAILEY SPENCER is, in the words
of her wife Elizabeth, an absolute
cloud of a girl. She is obsessed
with fairy tales and has an equally
passionate rivalry with ants. She
lives and writes in Seattle. For
more on Hailey and her work,
visit haileyspencerwrites.com

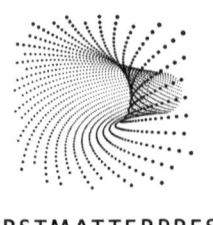

FIRSTMATTERPRESS
Portland, Ore.

First Matter Press is a collective press in Portland, Oregon, founded in 2018 to dissolve publication barriers for first-time publishing poets and genre-expanding writers. Our annual releases center community and craft by inviting authors into a creative cohort where they crystallize manuscripts in dialogue with editors and fellow writers and collaborate with featured artists on original cover art.

We are a 501(c)(3) non-profit organization and our authors maintain 100% copyrights and sales royalties of published work. Find our titles at IndieBound.org, Powells.com, BN.com and other major bookseller websites.

2022
FEATURED COVER ARTIST RACHEL MULDER

BETWEEN THESE BORDERS WANDERS A GOLEM
ahuva s. zaslavsky

EVEN THE AIR, TOO HEAVY
riley danvers

ONE ROW AFTER / BIR SIRA SONRA
sonya wohletz

SOMEONE I CAN HOLD GENTLY
xylophone mykland

STORIES FOR WHEN THE WOLVES ARRIVE
hailey spencer

FIRSTMATTERPRESS.ORG

2021
FEATURED COVER ARTIST ALEKSANDRA APOCALISSE

CONSIDER THE BODY, WINGED
jessica e. pierce

ROUTES BETWEEN RAINDROPS
dan wiencek

THE GROWTH LINES
gabby hancher

2020
FEATURED COVER ARTIST SARA SWOBODA

BODY UNTIL LIGHT
k.m. lighthouse

IT'S JUST YOU & ME, MISS MOON
emily moon

LOVERS AND OTHER STILL CREATURES
eitan codish

2019
FEATURED COVER ARTIST HELLSEA

OTHERWISE, MAGIC
lauren paredes

THE NIGHT SKY IS A PLACE WHERE THINGS GET LOST
andrew chenevert

TIME COUNTS BACKWARD FROM INFINITY
k.m. lighthouse

WE ARE NOT READY FOR WHAT WE ARE
ash good

2018
FEATURED COVER ARTIST HOLGER LIPPMANN

SOUNDS IN MY MÖBIUS MIND
ash good

YOU ARE AN AMBIGUOUS PRONOUN
k.m. lighthouse

www.ingramcontent.com/pod-product-compliance
Lightning Source LLC
Chambersburg PA
CBHW071159120626
46546CB00006B/2331